Food

PEAS

Louise Spilsbury

www.heinemann.co.uk/library
Visit our website to find out more information about Heinemann Library books.

To order:
☎ Phone 44 (0) 1865 888066
🗎 Send a fax to 44 (0) 1865 314091
🖥 Visit the Heinemann Bookshop at www.heinemann.co.uk/library to browse our catalogue and order online.

First published in Great Britain by Heinemann Library,
Halley Court, Jordan Hill, Oxford OX2 8EJ
a division of Reed Educational and Professional Publishing Ltd.
Heinemann is a registered trademark of Reed Educational and Professional Publishing Ltd.

OXFORD MELBOURNE AUCKLAND
JOHANNESBURG BLANTYRE GABORONE
IBADAN PORTSMOUTH (NH) USA CHICAGO

© Reed Educational and Professional Publishing Ltd 2002
The moral right of the proprietor has been asserted.

Designed by Celia Floyd
Illustrated by Alan Fraser
Originated by Ambassador Litho Ltd
Printed in Hong Kong/China by South China Printing Co.

ISBN 0 431 12773 5 (hardback)   ISBN 0 431 12778 6 (paperback)
06 05 04 03 02   06 05 04 03
10 9 8 7 6 5 4 3 2   10 9 8 7 6 5 4 3 2 1

British Library Cataloguing in Publication Data
Spilsbury, Louise
  Peas. – (Food)
  1. Peas 2. Juvenile literature
  I. Title
  641.3'5656

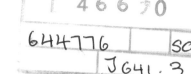

Acknowledgements
The Publishers would like to thank the following for permission to reproduce photographs:
Anthony Blake: p.10; Ardea: p.13; Corbis: pp.8, 9, 18; Findus: p.20; Gareth Boden: p.25; Holt Studios International: pp.4, 12, 14, 15, 16, 17, 19; Liz Eddison: pp.5, 6, 7, 21, 22, 23, 28 (left and right), 29 (top and bottom); Oxford Scientific Films: p.11; Stone: p.24.

Cover photograph reproduced with permission of Gareth Boden.

Every effort has been made to contact copyright holders of any material reproduced in this book.
Any omissions will be rectified in subsequent printings if notice is given to the Publishers.

CONTENTS

Words written in bold, **like this**, are explained in the Glossary.

WHAT ARE PEAS?

Peas are a kind of **vegetable**. A vegetable is a part of a plant that you can eat. Peas are the **seeds** of the pea plant.

Peas belong to a large **family** of plants called legumes. All legumes grow **pods**. Pods are long parcels that contain the plant's seeds.

KINDS OF PEAS

We eat many different kinds of peas, such as sugar peas, black-eyed peas and chickpeas. You eat the sugar pea **pods** as well as the peas.

sugar peas   black-eyed peas   chickpeas

These are green peas or garden peas. This book shows how farmers grow these peas and how they get from the field to your plate.

IN THE PAST

For thousands of years people have grown peas. The oldest pea ever found was 3000 years old. **Archaeologists** found it in South-East Asia.

When people went to the theatre or the races in ancient Rome, they ate fried peas as snacks. Would you like to eat fried peas instead of popcorn?

AROUND THE WORLD

In West Africa lots of people eat black-eyed peas. They make them into bean cakes, or cook them in a spicy sauce like this one.

Lots of people in China use sugar peas as an ingredient in their main meals. They are eaten whole with rice or noodles.

LOOKING AT PEA PLANTS

Pea plants have floppy **stems**. They have **tendrils** which wind round other plants to hold them up. Pea plants have flowers shaped like butterflies.

leaves

flower

stem

tendrils

After the flowers die, pea **pods** grow in their place. Pea pods keep the peas inside safe. The pods get bigger as the peas inside grow fatter.

13

GROWING PEAS

Farmers grow pea plants in huge fields. They use **ploughs** to break up the soil. This gets the soil ready for them to plant the **seeds**.

Farmers use a special machine to put the seeds into the soil. The machine puts the seeds just below the surface of the soil where peas grow best.

CARE OF PEA PLANTS

Pea plants do not grow well among **weeds**. Weeds are unwanted plants that grow quickly. Some farmers use sprays to get rid of weeds like these.

Insects and plant **diseases** can also damage pea plants. Many farmers also use special sprays to prevent these problems.

17

HARVESTING THE PEAS

When the peas are ready, farmers use machines to **harvest** (pick) them. Some machines only separate the **pods** from the **stems**.

Machines called **viners** take the peas
out of the pods as well. The viner
gently tumbles the pods about in a big
drum until the peas come out.

FROZEN AND TINNED PEAS

Many of the peas taken out of their **pods** are sold as **frozen** peas. They are frozen in an ice tunnel. Then they are packed into plastic bags.

Some peas are packed into tins with salt and water. Frozen peas and peas in tins keep longer than fresh peas.

EATING PEAS

To cook peas, you put them in boiling water for a few minutes. Lots of people eat cooked peas as a **vegetable** to have with a main meal.

Peas can also be cooked with other foods. People use peas in lots of **savoury** dishes, such as soups, stews and casseroles.

GOOD FOR YOU

Peas are good for you. When you eat them, your body uses the **vitamins** stored inside them. Vitamins help your body to grow and keep well.

Peas also contain **fibre**. Fibre is a part of some foods that passes through your body when you eat it. It helps keep your body healthy.

HEALTHY EATING

You need to eat different kinds of food to keep you well. This food pyramid shows you how much of each different food you need.

You should eat some of the things at the bottom and in the middle of the pyramid every day. Sweet foods are at the top of the pyramid. Try not to eat too many of these!

The food in each part of the pyramid helps your body in different ways.

Peas belong in the middle of the pyramid.

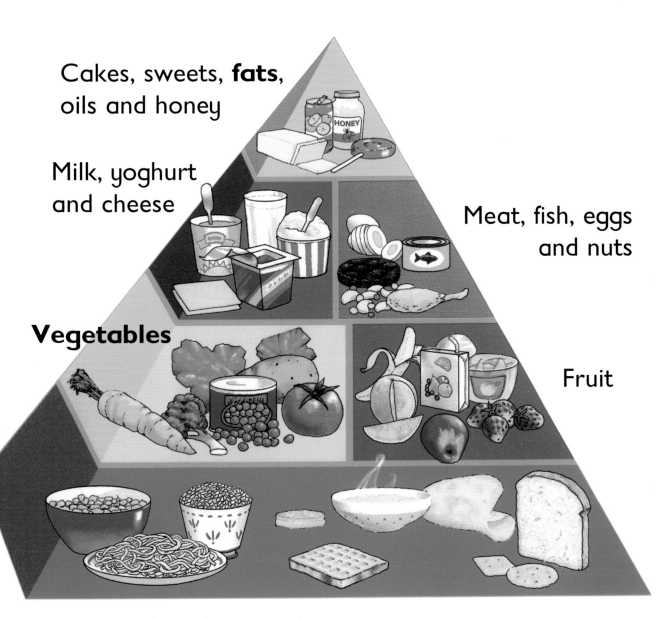

Cakes, sweets, **fats**, oils and honey

Milk, yoghurt and cheese

Meat, fish, eggs and nuts

Vegetables

Fruit

Bread, **cereals**, rice and pasta

27

PEA AND PASTA SALAD RECIPE

Ask an adult to help you with steps 1–4.

1 Cook the macaroni in boiling water for as long as it tells you on the packet.

2 Add the peas to the boiling water for the last 7 minutes.

You will need:
- 2 cups uncooked macaroni
- 1 small bag or box of frozen peas
- 150 g cheese
- 1 small onion
- $\frac{1}{2}$ cup mayonnaise

3 Drain the peas and macaroni in a colander.

colander

4 Grate the cheese and chop the onion into small pieces.

5 Put everything into a big bowl and stir in the mayonnaise.

6 Serve warm or cold.

GLOSSARY

archaeologist   person who finds out things about the past

cereals   grains like wheat and rice that are used to make flour, bread and breakfast foods

diseases   diseases can harm people, animals and plants. If a vegetable plant gets a disease, it may mean that its vegetables will not be good to eat.

family   group of plants or animals that are alike

fats   type of food. Butter, oil and margarine are kinds of fat.

fibre   part of a plant that passes through our bodies when we eat it

frozen   when food is kept as cold as ice to keep it fresh

harvest   when farmers or gardeners pick plants that they have grown

insect   small creature with six legs, like a beetle. Some insects eat plants and damage them.

plough   machine that breaks up the soil to make it loose and ready for planting seeds

pods   some plants grow their seeds inside pods. Pods are like little containers, which keep the seeds safe while they grow.

savoury   not sweet

seeds   made by the plant. Plants release seeds to grow into new plants.

stem   part of the plant that holds the leaves and flowers up to the light. Pea plants have floppy stems.

tendrils   special kind of leaves that grow very long and thin. They wrap themselves around other plants or sticks to help the pea plant stand up.

vegetable   part of a plant that we can eat. Vegetables include peas, carrots, potatoes and lettuce.

viner   farm machine that cuts pea plants and tumbles the pods gently to get the peas out of them

vitamins   food contains vitamins. Vitamins help us to grow and help us to stay well.

weeds   plants that grow quickly and in places where gardeners and farmers do not want them

31

MORE BOOKS TO READ

Plants: How Plants Grow, Angela Royston, Heinemann Library, 1999

Safe and Sound: Eat Well, Angela Royston, Heinemann Library, 1999

Senses: Tasting, Karen Hartley, Chris Macro, Phillip Taylor, Heinemann Library, 2000

The Senses: Taste, Mandy Suhr, Hodder Wayland, 1994

INDEX